SCHIRMER'S LIBRARY OF MUSICAL CLASSICS

Vol. 146

CARL CZERNY

Practical Method for Beginners on the Pianoforte

Op. 599

Edited, Revised and Fingered by

GIUSEPPE BUONAMICI

ISBN 978-0-7935-2567-6

G. SCHIRMER, Inc.

DISTRIBUTED BY
HAL•LEONARD®
CORPORATION
7777 W. BLUEMOUND RD. P.O. BOX 13819 MILWAUKEE, WI 53213

Practical Method for Beginners on the Pianoforte.

First Lessons
in learning the Notes.

C. CZERNY. Op. 599.

+) It is also well to practice the first 18 Exercises transposed a semitone higher and a semitone lower, retaining the original fingering.

Copyright © by G. Schirmer, Inc. (ASCAP) New York, NY
Printed in the U.S.A. by G. Schirmer, Inc.

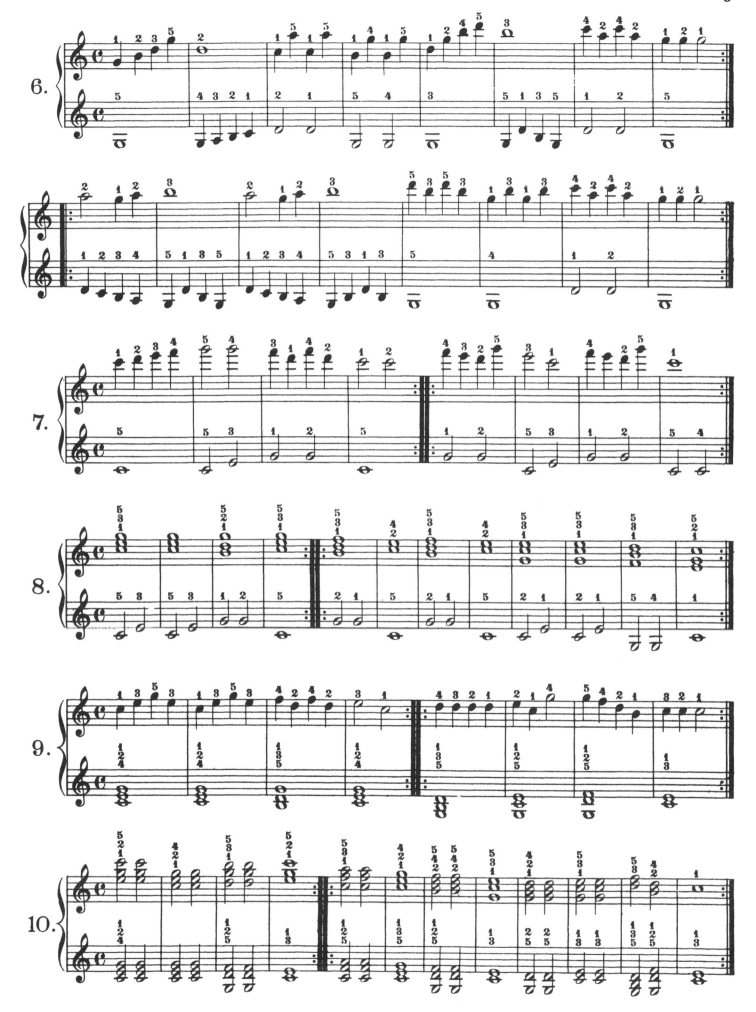

Five-finger Exercises
with quiet Hand.

+) Be careful to <u>hold</u> the first note of the measure, in the left hand, and to play the last *stuccato*.

+) Compare Remark to № 13.

17.

Exercises
within the Compass of an Octave, on white Keys only.

Exercises

exceeding the Compass of an Octave, but only on white Keys.

Exercises
for the Bass–Clef.

Exercises
with Sharps and Flats.

Exercises
in other easy Keys.

stacc. il basso.

Exercises
with Rests and other Signs.

Allegretto.

45.

Allegretto.

46.

p stacc. il basso.

Allegro.

47.

dolce.

48. Allegretto. *p* *f* Fine.

D.C. al Fine.

49. Allegro. *f* *sf*

D.C. al Fine.

Exercises
for the Attainment of Freedom and Agility.

+) Also practice a semitone higher, with the same fingering

++) Also transpose a semitone lower.

✝) Also practice in F♯, with a slight change of fingering in the 7th measure.

Vivace.

62.✝)

✝) Also practice in G♭.

65.✝)

Allegro.

✝) Also practice in D♭.

+) Also a semitone lower.

Allegretto.

68✝)

✝) May also be practiced a semitone higher and lower.

Allegretto.

69.

Allegro.

70.

Melodic Exercises
with and without Embellishments.

✢) Also practice in F♯

✳) Perform trill thus:

Allegretto.

76.

Andantino.

77⁺)

Allegretto.

+) Earlier way of using the dot; we should now write thus: etc:

Exercises

with Appoggiaturas and other useful Embellishments.

Allegretto all'Ungherese.

82.

Allegro.

83.

Allegro.

84.*)

*) Also transpose a semitone higher and lower.

Allegretto.

87.✝)

✝) Also transpose into F#, retaining the original fingering.

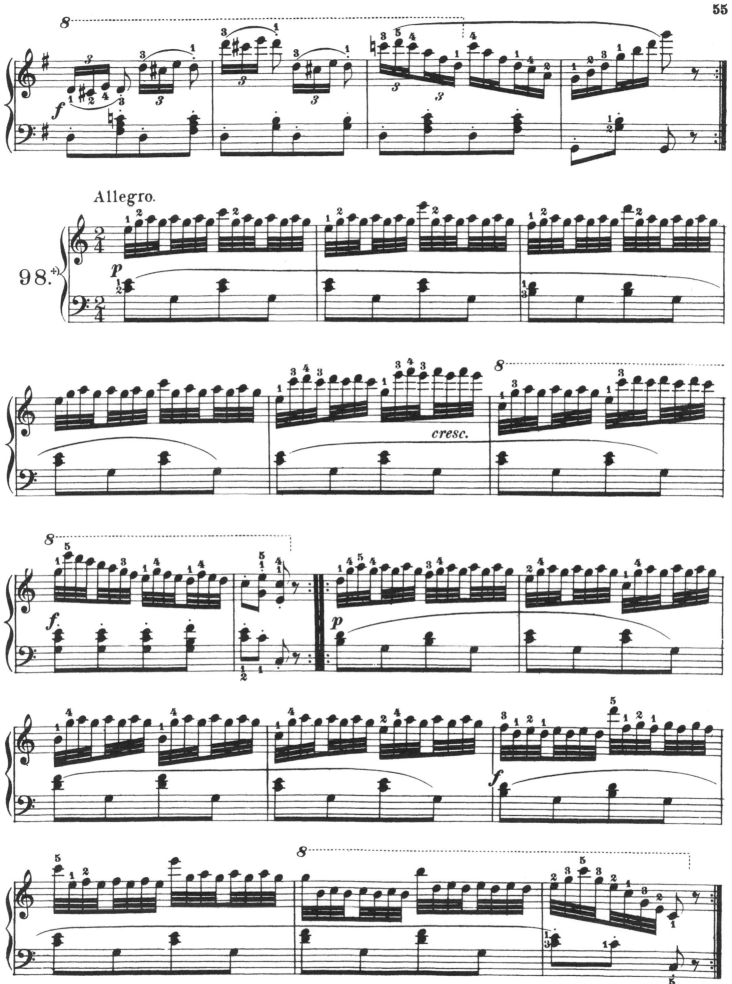

*⁺⁾ Also transpose a semitone higher and lower.